SUCHARIT

AYANAM

THE INCREDIBLE PATH

BlueRose ONE.co
Stories Matter
New Delhi • London

For permissions requests or inquiries regarding this publication,
please contact:

BLUEROSE PUBLISHERS
www.BlueRoseONE.com
info@bluerosepublishers.com
+91 8882 898 898
+4407342408967

ISBN: 978-93-5989-519-2

Cover design: Shivam
Typesetting: Namrata Saini

First Edition: January 2024

Dedication

Vakra-Tunndda Maha-Kaaya Suurya-Kotti Samaprabha |
Nirvighnam Kuru Me Deva Sarva-Kaaryessu Sarvadaa | |

I salute Vignaharta before penning more words about my book. In addition to salutations, I earnestly seek Lord Ganapati's blessings for the book, "Ayanam". I hope it sells thousands of copies and Ayanam connects with millions of readers' hearts.

I dedicate this book to my loving parents, family and friends living in India and abroad. To the precious readers and fantastic author buddies, thank you for always being there and encouraging me along the way. I thank everyone who invariably pushed me to attempt something distinct and to refine my words finer than the previous ones. Ultimately, it is for those who spend dull times hoping to encounter a speck of positivity and adventure someday.

To the beautiful girls, Archisha and Sulagna: You two made me switch from a voracious reader to a dedicated author. Thank you both for your criticism and motivation at the same time. Let's reach the sky, soaring with the book "Ayanam- The Incredible Path."

Acknowledgement

The quotes I wrote down in the last three years took a tangible form mainly due to Niladri. I sincerely thank "The Creative Circle's" founder, Niladri Shekhar Mitra, for thoroughly editing the work with tremendous patience. Niladri: without your guidance and brilliant suggestions, this book would not have seen the light.

The second one is for my Sanskrit Guru, Dr Bipin Bihari Satpathy, who helped me select the book's title. Thank you, sir, for the multiple suggested titles. Pexels and Pixbay websites, thank you for the lovely collection of images.

Besides thanking others, I owe my family and friends a lot. In the end, I am grateful to the lovely team of BlueRose Publications: you all did fantastic work, from formatting to cover designs. Namrata, Shivam, Shruti, Raghav and others, thank you guys.

Foreword

Dr. SITAKANT MAHAPATRA
Former Secretary, Culture, Govt. of India
Former President, UNESCO'S World Decade for Cultural Development

I have gone through the two anthologies of poems "Merak' and 'Estrenar' by Sucharita Parija. She has subtitled the latter as Beginning of a New Journey. I believe for a sincere poet, every poem is a new beginning. Such a poet is constantly trying to overcome oneself.

She has dedicated it to God: "Isavasyam Idam Sarvam." That happens to be my favourite line, which makes me dedicated to everything I do, be it poetry or everything I do during a day.

The poems in Estrenar I particularly liked are "Beginning of an End", and "Lonely". The latter is really a fine poem. Every poet knows that is the deep loneliness one feels the poems are born. In one of my longer poems "Birth of poetry," I have said as much. I have thought that a poet is capable of feeling this is the dry rituals of daily living. In that sense a poet is always alone, be it in a crowded street or in social conversations. She has a poem 'Believe on self'. That is a good beginning. One has to question oneself constantly and in that find solace and meaning of life.

Look deep inside yourself and constantly ask for meaning from the apparent meaninglessness of existence.

I wish Sucharita all the best.

Sitakant Mahapatra

Sraddha, 21 Satya Nagar, Bhubaneswar - 751 007
☎ (0674) 2570988 Mob 94377 78601 E-mail sitakantmahapatra@rediffmail com

Preface

"You will always remain motivated when you believe you must deliver your best in the future." -Suchi

The above quote exemplifies the daily inspiration or multi-vitamin I have been taking for many years through my words and thoughts. Happiness and Sadness are the sides of the coin named life, where one has importance because of the other.

Why did I write quotes in the first place? Quotes and Poetry have been embedded in my mind and heart since childhood. So, I had an idea to scribble down my thoughts whenever I had time, depending upon my mood. This book combines all my optimistic, upbeat, funny, heartbreaking, and blue moods into one.

One thought always circled over my head: how can I advise others without inspiring myself first? I needed to encourage myself through my positive vibes first thing in the morning. The seed of penning down the powerful quotes was planted in my mind to inspire me to sail through the day positively. Some days, it worked; however, many days, gloominess hovered in my life. This book is for you, me and thousands of readers who would find the quotes interesting and apply them in their lives.

Author Intro

Sucharita was born in Cuttack. She resides in the capital city of India. She has authored two poetry books and co-authored seven anthologies so far. Her debut book "Estrenar" has been translated into five foreign languages. Sucharita has been conferred with multiple awards for her two poetry books. She is a gold medalist and the CEMCA award winner at the post-graduation level, apart from graduating in Architecture.

Her book links are given below:
https://amzn.eu/d/8YxWyw5
and
https://amzn.eu/d/8YxWyw5.

Sucharita can be reached through:
www.streaksofsuchi.com
sucharitaparija15@gmail.com
www.instagram.com/streaksofsuchi
www.linkedin.com/in/sucharita-parija

Contents

Section-A

Life

"We are the nomads in life's travels."

**

"Life gives surprises at every moment."

**

"Fitness is a crucial feature of a healthy life."

**

"Savour life like your favourite food platter."

**

"Surprise your life by following its directions."

**

"Life gives surprises when we least expect them."

**

"Failure and success function as endless loops in life."

**

"Life will sail smoothly throughout the day with a smile."

**

"We all are born artists to perform on the stage called life."

**

"Life often traps you with its erratic moods and uncertainties."

**

"Every circumstance is transient throughout
our life's journey."

**

"Wisdom is the most eminent virtue to uphold
throughout life."

**

"In life, always hope for the best. But be prepared for the worst."

**

"Life bestows its blessings upon those who deserve
them the most."

**

"We are the designated travellers in the adventure
of life's journey."

**

"Life will evaporate like water in minutes without leaving a residue."

**

"Life surprises you when you are the least prepared for its surprises."

**

"Everything is transient in life, be it happy moments or sad incidents."

**

"Life is a journey being a fusion of satisfied and dissatisfied emotions."

**

"One can build a better or miserable life through thoughts and actions."

**

*"3 R's for charging your life vitality: **Revitalise, Reignite & Rejoice.**"*

**

"The most ruthless antagonist is none other than you in your life's occurrences."

**

"Life is a cycle of experiences. The beginning and the ending are unpredictable."

**

"Every person has infinite songs in their life. Each part of the song has an untold tale."

**

"Past mistakes may not define your life. But they will show you how to proceed in life."

**

"Our life is precisely like the moon. It begins from zero, and it ends in a complete phase."

**

"Stop being readily available for everyone in life. You will be the most miserable person on earth."

**

"As all fingers in the hands are different from each other,
all days in our life too are unique in their way."

**

"Smile at everyone every day without reason. Life will be more
gratifying for you as well as for others."

**

"Everything is transient in life except the right decisions taken by
one. It will cling to one's self Forever."

**

"Life teaches you the most valuable lessons at unexpected
moments by unusual persons and in unforeseen circumstances."

**

"Life will be only black or white without multiple hues of
colours. Well, black and white are also
detected in the colour palette."

**

Motivational

"Love yourself first.
Be happy with yourself.
You complete yourself."

**

"Let each day bring new goals."

**

"Greed leads to destruction in life."

**

"We are the heroes of our own lives."

**

"You are the best reviewer of your character."

**

"Feel young in the mind to keep illnesses at bay."

**

"Heaven resides inside our soul: the haven for bliss."

**

"School: Where one gets a glimpse of the real world."

**

"Let one face light with a smile each day of their life."

**

"Admire your strengths and correct your deficiencies."

**

"Victory over one's mind is the greatest victory in life."

**

"Every day is a new day to begin your work differently."

**

"Believe in yourself first before trusting another person."

**

"The most vital ingredient of home-cooked food is love."

**

"Our hand displays the best example of unity in variety."

**

11

'You deserve the utmost respect and love from yourself."

**

"All labour done with dignity by anyone is actual labour."

**

"You are doing yourself a favour by staying honest within."

**

"An angry person can never reach great heights in their life."

**

"Sports de-stresses the body, and meditation calms the mind."

**

"If one wants to be happy, nobody can stop them. Be happy!"

**

"Do not be the servant of wealth – command it like a master."

**

"Listen to your inner self often and walk on your chosen path."

**

"Bury the distress and nightmares in the previous year's grave."

**

"Welcome a change in your life and see how it transforms you."

**

"Push yourself to conquer your fears. Be your true
motivator in life."

**

"Mirror and trust are identical. Once broken,
both are beyond repair."

**

"Let go of yesterday so you can embrace tomorrow
without inhibition."

**

"The suppressed bitterness that weighs heavily erupts in
various forms."

**

"Betrayal by someone close is the most shocking blow
a person can get."

**

13

"Give yourself another chance to succeed over
the depression in your life."

**

"Repeat the words: 'I am happy from within' multiple times in
the morning."

**

"The goal in life is to live. So, live with happiness.
No space left for regret."

**

"Let thousands of Diyas take the darkness of
ignorance away from our minds."

**

"One's real strength lies in one's mind.
Hence, the mind should be recharged."

**

"When the mind is calm, and the body is still,
seek solutions to your problems."

**

"A new beginning is feasible only when a former
beginning has come to an end."

**

"The ultimate goal is not to seek nirvana but to attain the state
of realisation: You."

**

"Food prepared by oneself is the healthiest, most hygienic, and
safest to consume."

**

"If you missed the first chance, then do not cry. There is always a
second chance."

**

"Seek to learn from the adversities in life. Opportunities will
knock at your door."

**

"Suicide is never the solution to all tangible and intangible
problems in life's path."

**

"Live your life on your terms and conditions. Believe in yourself in the first place."

**

"Live life on your terms and conditions. It will be more comfortable in the long run."

**

"You are the most loyal friend of yours. Adhere to your inner trustworthiness in life."

**

"Humour is by far the best medicine for chronic patients diagnosed with gloominess."

**

"Fall in love with yourself in the first place before falling in love with someone else."

**

"One can conquer the world with hard work, endearing expressions, and humbleness."

**

*"The only place where emotions overflow,
and love spreads to every corner is Home."*

**

*"Hang on till the end in a failed situation in
life to find the light of hope at the end of it."*

**

*"You are the best critic of your personality.
Do not be too gentle or too harsh on yourself."*

**

*"My resolution for the next day: I do not wish to
make false promises to myself or others."*

**

*"Who is the creator of all our pain? Our mind.
Let's remove all negativity from our minds."*

**

*"You are the commander-in-chief of your life. Remember,
everything is in your own hands."*

**

"A short-tempered man loses his emotional and physical power due to his negative emotions."

**

"You are proficient in writing your memoir. Discover your soul and pen down your life story."

**

"You will always remain motivated when you believe you must deliver your best in the future."

**

"Believe in yourself. Listen to your inner voice. Then, you will emerge as a miracle on your own."

**

"Listen to your heart amidst the tranquillity of your mind; your queries will be answered quickly."

**

"New beginnings are gateways to numerous dreams: To experience, explore, and appreciate each day."

**

"Progress may not occur from one's comfort zone. Leave the bubble of familiarity to progress in life."

**

"Anger is the collection of numerous pains within oneself, often bursting at the wrong place and time."

**

"No one can bring you happiness from the outside. You can only download it from your own mind."

**

"Connectivity with technology is immeasurable. It should not be a source of discontentment in one's life."

**

"Determination is the key to accomplishment in life. Be inspired by your inner voices, and stay motivated."

**

"Self-cheating bursts out in the worst way and at the worst moment in life. So be honest with yourself."

**

"A new beginning may be planned in the future. Hang on for a little longer rather than hanging yourself."

**

"Each failure in our lives empowers us to grasp one thing emphatically – there is always scope for improvement."

**

"The spirit is accessible from the birth-death cycle. We interact through the soul to reach the spirit and refine it."

**

"Proceed forward with a revitalised power even if you see just a flickering light at the far end of the darkness."

**

"Every day brings a different challenge in life. It is up to you to decide whether to fly in the sky or sink in the sea."

**

"Sunshine flutters her wings excitedly in every direction after the storm recedes. So be the sunshine in your turbulent life."

**

"The triumph of good over evil invariably happens in life. Never lose hope when harmful elements cover your life's sky."

**

"I am striving hard with faith to ascend the stairs to heaven. I have countless blessings to cross the hurdle at heaven's gate."

**

"Embrace yourself without any inhibitions but with all flaws. You will then catch a glimpse of the best version of yourself."

**

"Nobody can duplicate, multiply, curtail, or improve your life. The only authoritative person in your life is you yourself."

**

"Time is the most incredible healer in life for infinite despair, failures, and hardships administered through body and mind."

**

"Be grateful for catching the lovely colour of the sunset. It gives hope that you will see the resurgence of your life the next day."

**

"Beneath each piece of poetry rests an extension of interwoven emotions. Poets are sentimental blockheads."

**

"Your failure and success in life are your own. Neither condemn others for your loss nor ignore to appreciate others' support."

**

"It is never too late, and you are never too old to embark on a new journey if you are soaked in passion and vitality to do it."

**

"New beginnings are forever challenging to commence. Occasionally, we must figure out when and where to begin a new life."

**

"Dream about today all day through. Plan to complete the work today. Today is in our grasp; let it not move away from our clasp."

**

"Our mind is the powerhouse in our lives. We can banish evil thoughts from it and restrain it from wandering. It's all in our hands."

**

"Remain cool like ice from outside. Retain the fire in life glowing from within. Remember this mantra to achieve success in life."

**

"Refrain from settling for something that does not create excitement within you. Be it in your hobbies or your career choices."

**

"Choose a career of your choice and not one that's decided by others. You have the ambition and vision to make it extraordinary."

**

"We should strive to return to the world with full vigour after a tragedy or failure as the Phoenix rises from her predecessor's ashes."

**

"Each day should be a new beginning—no burden to carry from yesterday, no pondering about what's going to happen tomorrow."

**

"Hard work and consistency are the keys to opening the doors of achievement. May good luck be with you in your quest for Success."

**

"Never forgive the most trusted person in your life who had the power to betray you at your back. But, who gave them the strength to destroy you?"

**

"If someone leaves you for any flimsy reason, let them go from your life. But do not sit back and cry. It is better to continue your life with yourself."

**

"Nobody on this Earth has the power to alter your perception of you without your authorisation. Love one individual the most in your life – yourself."

**

"Water droplets are the main elements that create rain. Similarly, anger is the primary ingredient for a miserable life, bursting out when it becomes weighty."

**

"Today is distinct from yesterday. Tomorrow will be replaced today in due time. We should strive to live each day separately, without looking back or forward."

**

Society

"Society has no existence without people."

**

"Love or hate society, but one cannot ignore it."

**

"Strive to stay away from toxic people and a hypercritical society."

**

"Society abandons an individual when that person needs it the most."

**

"Truth, non-violence, simplicity, and humanity can never go outdated in society or life."

**

"Some traditions need to change with time. Only then will our society evolve and thrive."

**

"Stop condemning society. If you are correct, then do not pay any heed to society's blabbers."

**

"Each woman is a warrior in her unique way. She fights her demons every day to be accepted by society."

**

"The fire of a genuine heart can never get doused by the water of anybody's criticism or society's rejection."

**

"Society consists of several hypercritical and insane people. Their response and opinions change according to circumstances."

**

"Religion does not separate one from the masses. Certain narrow-minded people of society create separation in other's minds."

**

"Society and people are the two sides of a coin. They can neither survive without one another nor breathe the same air with each other."

**

"The community as a whole serve as a giant cage. It is better not to get trapped in it. You may be held captive there for life if you give in to its whims."

**

"Doctors, police, scientists, teachers, and nurses are the original celebrities of our society. We must recognise and appreciate them for their endless dedication."

**

Laughter & Smiles

"Smile forever, as it costs nothing."

**

"Laughter is the best painkiller you can have."

**

"Laugh alone or with someone, but do it daily."

**

"One smile lights up the entire face and keeps one happy."

**

"Sound sleep is the best medicine ever, just like laughter."

**

"A smile is highly contagious and spreads as fast as a forest fire."

**

"Smile without any reason. It will shift a lousy
mood into a good one."

**

"Life's journey will be smooth if you have loads of laughter in your daily diet."

**

"A smile is the most infectious disease that spreads even faster than the forest fire."

**

"Smile is the best medicine that spreads sunshine, mindfulness, ingenuity, love, and exhilaration."

**

Inspirational

"Our thoughts shape our destiny."

**

"The best is waiting to be uncovered."

**

"The failures of my past are now my strength."

**

"One should write their own inspirational story."

**

"To be an honest individual takes much courage."

**

"Keep moving in life even if you slip on the path."

**

"You are both the hero and the villain of your life."

**

"Miracles are taking place every waking hour in our lives."

**

"Move on from disturbances that conceal your true identity."

**

"It is essential to build one's integrity and shape one's character."

**

"Be the light yourself instead of seeking a light in the darkness."

**

"I aspire to continue as myself and not change myself for anyone."

**

"Leave your footprints on the beach, even if it stays for just a minute."

**

"Patience is the only word that is synonymous with Gautama Buddha."

**

"Each failure brings a new lesson that must always be remembered."

**

"I prefer not to explain myself to the world. I am not there to be judged by others."

**

"The best gift you can give yourself is to forgive others and step out of the past's door."

**

"Spread the essence of positivity on the path you travel, physically or emotionally, daily."

**

"It is essential to learn to fight for yourself. This interpretation is the biggest lesson in life."

**

"There will be no sorrow, suffering, and despair if we do not expect anything from anyone."

**

"My best is yet to come": "This should be the tagline in life to put more effort into one's passion."

**

"One can never escape from grief and hurtful words. So, strive to blow them away like bubbles in your life."

**

"Many times, victory can be accomplished with love and patience, instead of bloodshed and brutality."

**

"Proceed forward with a revitalised power even if you see a just flickering light at the far end of the darkness."

**

"It is not wise to crumble under a series of disturbing episodes. Pause, believe in yourself, and then march ahead."

**

"A new morning is waiting in slumber for your good thoughts to wake it up and make it unforgettable."

**

"One's personality is reflected through one's words and actions. Spread love and kindness in this world of misery and brutality."

**

"Adversities and hardships should be greeted with open arms as they introduce you to and teach you the most significant life lessons."

**

"Let every minute be like a festival overfilled with colours of sound health, endless happiness, evergreen love, and eternal peace throughout the globe."

**

Humour

"Negative is a wrong term in life.
Only sometimes...
Being Covid negative is a gift."

**

"My mind stays full but always filled with junk."

**

"I had a dream to expand my horizons in life.
Only my waist grabbed my plans."

**

"Dinner feels wonderful at exotic locations when someone
else is footing the bill."

**

"You know you have entered mid-life when neighbours invite you
for religious functions over a wild party."

**

"My friend is a great dancer when he drinks. Alcoholics often
forget things and repeat the same activities. Did I tell you about
my friend who dances? I keep forgetting things."

**

Spiritual

"Meditation is food for a blossoming of the soul."

**

"Devotion unfastens the hinges of divine blessings."

**

"One's state of peace resides in one's inner chamber."

**

"Humanity is above any religion in the whole universe."

**

"God is the most elevated Spiritual Master in the universe."

**

"Worship and prayers are the direct paths that lead to God."

**

"God showers His blessings to every individual in various ways."

**

"Keeping calm and silent is the most straightforward path to reaching God."

**

"God is omnipresent. Meditate with a calm mind. Get your
doubts cleared."

**

"Let the Diyas glow bright and bring happiness to every home
every evening!"

**

"Let the fire of a Diya burn all negativity within us every
morning and evening."

**

"A person who evaluates himself before he judges others is
genuinely religious."

**

"If one believes in himself first, then he is the most notable
spiritual person in the world."

**

"God is scheduling and rescheduling your necessities all day long.
Have patience!"

**

"Sometimes, the path to obtaining blessings from God is forged with doubt and restlessness."

**

"God is the most outstanding director of all time. Have patience, and never doubt God's work!"

**

"Lord Ganesh is also known as the remover of the obstacles hindering your path to success in life."

**

"When one is pushed into a pit of despair, God sends a rope for them to clutch it and climb back up."

**

"God is the best planner for every being existing in the universe. Never doubt His blessings and plans."

**

"God is steadily standing behind you, emitting His powerful energy. Immerse yourself in God's blessings!"

**

"Pray in silence to seek the answer. Silence is the best choice during an hour of crisis with chaotic thoughts."

**

"Thank the Almighty every morning for providing you with another day to accomplish your dreams in life."

**

"One can be physically, emotionally, and intellectually tired at times. The soul, however, never gets exhausted."

**

"The explored path will be smooth without snags if one has strong willpower, God's grace, and inherent potential."

**

"If someone conquers one's self, that will be the most significant triumph ever—the most excellent teaching of Buddha."

**

"Silent prayer reaches God faster than chanting mantras. Heed the change in your life, and stay grateful to the Almighty."

**

"God has many forms. The style of worshipping God also differs. But He showers His blessings in only one direction and for all."

**

"The route from "hopeless" to "reasonable" crosses through God. He remembers when, where, and how to answer one's prayers."

**

"Listen, 'Mr /Ms Challenges,' you can enter my life whenever you like. I have God's blessings and strength to defeat you anytime."

**

"You can often not decide what to do on your own. Transfer the work into the account of God. He is the best director and banker in the universe."

**

"Remember not to underestimate the power of prayer, faith, love, and blessings! They will make the pathway from unfeasible to feasible for you."

**

"We should pray to the Almighty to bestow us with the strength to fight our problems and pain every day instead of begging Him to remove them from our lives instantly."

**

Observations & Musings

"What is more painful?
Betrayal of a friend
Or
Trusting them unthinkingly?"

**

"What is more heart-breaking?
Exploitation by a total stranger
Or
Indifference of a loved one."

**

"Eat healthy food to survive."

**

"Do not be a prisoner of greed."

**

"Tomorrow is the future of today."

**

"In every new front lies an ending."

**

"Our future leans upon us today."

**

"Time is the real wealth in one's life."

**

"Trust is silent till someone breaks it."

**

"Is sorry the opposite word of love?"

**

"P- Power

O- Of

E- Enigmatic

M- Movements

S- Satisfies Soul

They cruise silently in life's ocean."

**

"What is Beauty?
It's nothing but the following:
B- Beginning and
E- Ending of
A- A
U- Universal
T- Truth about
Y- You."

**

"Heaven is not the final destination.
It is a stopover in the journey of life."

**

"The ego is the core reason for distress."

**

"Where my heart dwells is my "Home"."

**

"My silence speaks volumes about me."

**

"Never murder your conscience in life.
Do not indulge in unethical practices."

**

"Never get afraid of new phases in life."

**

"Who has caught a glance at the future?
It is better to shape the present moment."

**

"Does loneliness make way for creativity?
Or
Are creative folks lonely by choice?"

**

"A fantastic person is fearless at heart."

**

"Betrayal is a frightening sort of emotion."

**

"Safety is not only important, it is crucial."

**

"Let some secrets stay buried deep inside."

**

"Doctors are living Gods in the universe."

**

"Relationship takes the path that life directs."

**

"An angry person is a miserable one in life."

**

"Water is our life's most crucial component."

**

*"Home is not layered with bricks and mortar.
But with vast respect and consistent effort."*

**

"Behind each song lies an unexplored story."

**

"An optimistic mind attracts positive energy."

**

"Save good feelings from evil thoughts in life."

**

"Self-love is not the alternate word for selfish."

**

"A mirror reflects the true self of an individual."

**

"Home is the place where I grew up with love."

**

"I have one regret in life, which is uncountable."

**

"One's inner feelings get reflected on their faces."

**

"Every disappointment teaches us a new lesson."

**

"Surprises arrive every waking hour in our lives.
To feel delighted or disappointed is our choice."

**

"Loyalty to any profession is rare and admirable."

**

"Talk to yourself first – The new trend of today."

**

"Wisdom is the collection of lifelong knowledge."

**

"Occasionally, being alone refuels vitality in life."

**

"Refrain from eating unhealthy food all the time."

**

"Behind every pain, many blessings are hidden."

**

"An angry person hurts himself more than others."

**

"Obsession can destroy or preserve a competition."

**

"Selfish people solely concentrate on themselves."

**

"An angry person is their own greatest antagonist."

**

"A pet is the best therapist who listens to only you."

**

"Animals conduct themselves as per their wishes."

**

"Animals speak through their facial expressions."

**

"Hatred is a strong emotion in life that runs deep."

**

"Self-love is not a crime but the need of the hour."

**

"If you do not follow time, it will never listen to you."

**

"Is it a myth or a fact that "April Fool's Day" exists?"

**

"Everything appears unique when the mind is calm."

**

"Be optimistic today! Stay satisfied at the moment."

**

"Traditional education makes one literate, not wise."

**

"The ego is the vicious energy behind every downfall."

**

"Any mastery in the world falls in the category of art."

**

"Gratitude is the most potent feeling a person can have."

**

"Do I need to crush my desires to gain vain popularity?
Do I need to sacrifice love to advance in my career?"

**

"Bollywood is the ultimate destination for movie buffs."

**

"Every single person is born an artist with their style."

**

"Victory is attained by those who do not fear failure."

**

"Sports is an integral piece of physical growth in life."

**

"Lies do not fly on their own. Liars give them wings."

**

"Change is the only perpetual constant in the universe."

**

"Nobody can take away whatever is stored in one's luck."

**

"Science has carried us to the moon but not to our souls."

**

"S - Stationery

C - Close Friends

H - Happiness

O - Opportunity

O - Outfits

L – Laughter"

All of these are available under one roof named "school."

**

"Being humble is one of many strengths a person owns."

**

"The link we need in today's time is through Empathy."

**

"Empathy is a unique trait that can transform the world."

**

"Fight, but for your rights, not just for the sake of action."

**

"A relationship is like a mirror. It reflects the exact image of it."

**

"Nothing seems impossible for a fearless person on Earth."

**

"Obsession with anything is not a boon but a bane in life."

**

"Is technology the saviour or the antagonist in our lives?"

**

"Life begins on the Earth and completes its journey on it."

**

"We travel through our minds at our every waking moment."

**

"Beware of fulfilling the demands of self-indulgent people."

**

"The world is the base for your climbing to attain success."

**

"How do you draw the line between imagination and reality?"

**

"Love and compassion are the genuine traits of a gentleman."

**

"Progress will only be made with a stable and persistent mind."

**

"Betrayal by a friend is the worst heartbreak anyone can face."

**

"A nurse nourishes her patient back to life, just like a mother."

**

"The ego is the most prominent antagonist in everyone's life."

**

"Every lying leads to desolation. Be extra cautious about lies!"

**

"Every person has infinite songs in their life – the untold ones."

**

"I am invariably stressed out in order to keep others stress-free."

**

"Every morning, I look like I am on a rollercoaster of emotions."

**

"Five Keys to Unlock the Door of Success in Life:
Determination, discipline, dexterity, dedication, and diligence."

**

"An old memory must be sealed correctly for a fresh beginning."

**

"Being lonely inside a crowded room is the worst feeling in life."

**

"The moon is the reflection of imperfection with perfection in life."

**

"Count your blessings one by one. Discard the thorns that prick."

**

"It is better to avoid fulfilling the demands of self-indulgent ones."

**

"Everything has the same inception, but the end is different for all."

**

"What is education? Does it give you clarity or clutter your mind?"

**

"We successfully keep on covering our pain, but our eyes never lie."

**

"We all can transform the nation through
single acts of kindness."

**

"Death is not the final terminus. It is a transit in the soul's journey."

**

"Sometimes, raindrops fall on Earth as blessings from the Almighty."

**

"Kindness is the worthiest wealth that will remain with you forever."

**

"The beginning is a beautiful vision that lasts forever in our minds."

**

"Adventure is an emotion embedded in everyone's mind by default."

**

"Relax while you can; Life is too unpredictable to plan for the future."

**

"Let the rays of positive thoughts clear the gloomy
air of life's reality."

**

"It's not anyone's mistake that people break up with their loved ones."

**

"Loyalty becomes invisible once its identity is
in crisis or is misused."

**

"In challenging circumstances, a person's natural
character is revealed."

**

"The cloud of delusion invariably surrounds the
knowledgeable world."

**

"Multi-tasking is an art that can be achieved by
few men and women."

**

"How does one deal with the betrayal? Retaliate or
forgive the person?"

**

"One's perspective towards life is the outcome of wisdom and education."

**

"The same technologies we feel proud of inventing have imprisoned us."

**

"The person who attempts to tame and train his mind is a winner in life."

**

"The words 'miss you' are not mere words but a vessel full of emotions."

**

"Falling in love makes you strong. Falling out of love shatters your heart."

**

"Communication is the heart of any personal or professional relationship."

**

"Time is the best healer, but the duration of that time is yet to be revealed."

**

"One's progress is counted by inner strength rather than outward success."

**

"Never make a promise you cannot fulfil, be it to yourself or your children."

**

"Do not leap into the web of an unknown darkness by committing suicide."

**

"You are only a dedicated disciple if past mistakes have taught you lessons."

**

"Genuine personalities do not hide behind masks of honey-dripping words."

**

"An educated person holds the power to distinguish between right and wrong."

**

"A staunchly religious person always follows their religion without realising."

**

"One should steadfastly believe in life's turbulent and intermittent moments."

**

"The doctors are the incarnations of God. We can at least show respect to them."

**

"We pursue attaining peace endlessly, disregarding the analysis of our minds."

**

"It is better to stay healthy in mind and body rather than landing in the hospital."

**

"Feelings can be a platter that ranges from pleasant dreams to obnoxious folks."

**

"A person who takes risks in life with firm feet and a calm mind is a brave one."

**

"Life seems either black or white when looked through the eyes of a simpleton."

**

"May positive thoughts take the darkness away from our lives at every second!"

**

"Progress is not the outcome of one day but many years of consistent hard work."

**

"A person with profound wisdom listens to everything with attention and patience."

**

"The world is a camp where people stay and leave according to pre-appointments."

**

"With the cooperation of members in a team, the results will invariably be a win."

**

"An ordinary person becomes a hero when he turns his weakness into his strength."

**

"Strength displays the actual colour of a person while facing hardship and struggle."

**

"One should listen to their subconscious thoughts throughout their entire lifetime."

**

"One's day is a day to relax till the end, relearn old ones, and rejuvenate the energy."

**

"The true essence of celebration lies in blissfulness and in a peaceful environment."

**

"Age is not always a sign of maturity. It just is a branch in the tree of life's journey."

**

"Death is not the final destination. It is an ongoing journey till the soul goes to rest."

**

"The nurse is an expression that simultaneously represents firmness and gentleness."

**

"The courage to face every adversity is a hidden weapon every human possesses."

**

"Doctors and Mothers are divinity embedded within. They save lives or create lives."

**

*"Older people feel lonely as younger ones spare less time
for them in today's rat race."*

**

*"All inconsiderate people on the planet, kindly refrain
from entering my precious life."*

**

*"Forbearance can lead to hitting the jackpot or
ruining all the effort one makes in life."*

**

*"My life is a collection of muddling thoughts weighing
me down with their heaviness."*

**

*"If we can understand a fraction of science today,
we can create marvels the next day."*

**

*"Bravery is a hidden inner strength.
It pours out effortlessly at the right time and place."*

**

"The courage to face every adversity is the most powerful emotion that anyone can have."

**

"One can never control the creative urge that rushes in the veins of creative intellectuals."

**

"There exists a hidden child in every individual, be it an Octogenarian or a Vigintennial."

**

"Meeting young and energetic minds, irrespective of physical age, is always rejuvenating."

**

"Humans are unique museums. Multitudes of emotions have been assembled in one place."

**

"Those who befriend animals quickly live in peace as they have connected with souls better."

**

"Sunshine is the best medicine one can have and it is also available to everyone in abundance."

**

"My reflection is my best buddy. She laughs and cries with me when everyone else goes away."

**

"Is the large balcony of a house directly proportional to the generous nature of its occupants?"

**

"We should not allow technology to control our lives and overpower our thought processes."

**

"The most loyal and everlasting companion one could ever reach out to in this universe is one's pet."

**

"Trust is the foundation of every relationship. Especially the bond between a husband and wife."

**

"Take good care of yourself. Then, sit back and observe
how you bloom into a beautiful flower."

**

"There is a difference between sacrifice by self and self-love.
Self-love is greater than self-sacrifice."

**

"It is better to pay attention to yourself at regular intervals
than to fulfil the endless demands of others."

**

"The ways of life are beyond human comprehension.
Progressing with the flow is always helpful."

**

"It takes just a minute to condemn others.
However, it takes ages to own up to your own mistake."

**

"We are real-life actors ready to enact various roles.
We get applauded or criticised, depending on our performance."

* *

"Opening and closing is a never-ending loop.
A new beginning is the endpoint of the former entry."

**

"Everyone welcomes the rain after a scorching day. It brings joy
and a smile to everyone's face."

**

"Heaven is where my family and soul mates coexist in harmony.
Can heaven be found on Earth?"

**

"Do not worship the single idol installed outdoors. But the soul
that resides deep within oneself."

**

"A positive attitude gives rise to hope, which can transform goals
and ambitions to likely from unlikely."

**

"Anniversaries mean remembering a significant occurrence in
one's life that might be sunny or bleak."

**

"My thoughts are like tiny thorns. They prick at the wrong time and are unmindful of my feelings."

**

"An enemy can neither destroy us without our acknowledgement nor support us without our consent."

**

"Wisdom is the most potent weapon of human beings. Therefore, it should never be misused by anyone."

**

"Refrain from expecting anything from anyone, no matter how difficult it might be to get into that state."

**

"My silence can be because of my anger, anxiety, bitterness, and sorrow. It is never because of my loneliness."

**

"Tomorrow will be a new beginning in life. It will be the end of today's unhappiness and uncertainty."

**

"Our mind is the powerhouse of peace. We need to channel our restless minds to attain peace all the time."

**

"Today's youth feels abandoned at most times as they do not live in the real world surrounded by real people."

**

"Distance yourself from negative thoughts and cynical people. Life will be peaceful and content for you."

**

"My silence can be because of my anger, anxiety, bitterness, and sorrow. It is never because of my loneliness."

**

"As work outlines a vital role in every human being's life, one should embrace one's duty without grumbling."

**

"Forgive your enemy, not because they deserve it but to overcome your own hostile and harmful feelings."

**

"Blessings are links between Heaven and the Hell. Blessed are those who are ready for the harsh battles in life."

**

"A beginning always looks more attractive than the end. Many times, new beginnings are depressing to begin."

**

"The future looks successful when it combines today's careful strategy with the learnings from yesterday's errors."

**

"Forgiveness is the most potent weapon of an individual. One who forgives has the ultimate control over themselves."

**

"The invention of technology is the most significant benefit. But being a captive of technology is the most annoying bit."

**

"Those who have helped me meet my inner self are my Gurus. So, I bow my head before my masters every morning."

**

"Each murderer has a story to reveal about his intention for the murder. Seldom it's real, and often, it's not correct."

**

"Accidents and viruses may not destroy a person. But grief and helplessness will kill a person instantly from within the body."

**

"The eyes are the key to the threshold of the heart. Close your eyes and lead the way to unravel the mysteries of the cosmos."

**

"One's religion should be one's sole right. It cannot be used as an influence to spread resentment among humankind."

**

"Education, money, or success does not stay for eternity. Rather, it is the essence of an individual that lingers forever."

**

"A man with immense riches is never an independent person. He is and will stay a captive of his own wealth till he realises it."

**

"Problems bang impatiently on my door every morning. Shall I let them set their foot inside my heart or turn a deaf ear to them?"

**

"All individuals are a part of royalty without a distinct kingdom. Everyone should wear a crown with tolerance and humility in mind."

**

"A simple lifestyle can give liberation from the most potent of enemies. It's a model our father of the nation displayed to the entire world."

**

"The journey between **the impossible and the possible is determined more by one's subconscious** than their conscious mind."

**

"It is hard to accept the failures that are thrown at your path out of the blue. But once you get it, life becomes a lot easier to live."

**

"People often push through the crowd, adding to the distress of an already chaotic traffic. Do they do it deliberately or just out of habit?"

**

"Cinema portrays human emotions from multiple perspectives. Good cinema can motivate one in life, but it's rare to find good cinema today."

**

"Eyes exhibit the innermost emotions of a person. Our smile can be artificial, or words may sound harsh, but the eyes always reflect our true feelings."

**

"How do you feel when someone trashes your loving creation so carelessly to satisfy their endless ego? Well, he is not in my elite league of reflection."

**

"The faces of fake people are always covered with multiple lies. They hang around to witness your downfall, not your success. Keep your distance from these people."

**

"We can spread immense blessings everywhere if we throw even a small pinch of kindness daily into the world like a tiny pebble that can generate infinite waves."

**

Nature & Environment

"Sunshine represents hope and positivity."

**

"Sunshine is the best therapist one can get."

**

"The greatest treasure for all of us is nature."

**

"Nature's silence is the most powerful medium."

**

"Misfortune strikes when nature breaks its silence."

**

"Leave the planet Earth in a stable form for future generations."

**

"To live in harmony with the environment and ourselves is an art."

**

"The summer has a distinct flavour. Soak in the sunshine of summer."

**

"Global Warming is the most visible consequence of
human greed and negligence."

**

"Please save planet Earth. We do not aspire to be
the last generation here."

**

"Nature gives a better connection to human beings
than any modern device."

**

"Mother Earth loves her children selflessly.
We are her unkind and ungrateful brats."

**

"Nature is the best mentor in the universe.
It teaches through action and not by words."

**

"Human greediness has shattered Mother Earth.
Let her recover on her own by giving her rest."

**

"The Earth requires silence and rest at this time of transition. Show respect to Mother Earth now."

**

"The latest disaster of humankind is Global Warming. It is by the people and against the people."

**

"We should be obliged to our planet for giving us a place to live, and must safeguard it from every infliction."

**

"The tree stands quietly and provides us with everything it can. Never hurt nature's elements or be ready to face her fury."

**

"Calamities, epidemic, global warming, environment: These are the consequences of Mother Nature's silent tears."

**

"Mother Earth is benevolent enough to give us refuge. We must reciprocate her generosity and not destroy her resources."

**

"Mother Nature dotes on her children with lots of forbearances.
So show respect and give back love to her in all possible manners."

**

"Trees and mothers are alike in various forms. They shield, support,
nourish, and embrace their children in silence. Respect both in life."

**

"Nature is the best creation of the Almighty. But humans are
trying to modify nature as per their needs and mess with its
natural beauty."

**

"Humans are the most intelligent species available on this Earth.
They need to preserve nature and its components like plants,
wildlife and water bodies."

**

"After a stormy night, the sun shines brilliantly, dispelling the darkness."

**

Section-B

Women

"Women are the architects of the world."

**

"Perfection is the other name of a woman."

**

"Women function as the strongest pillars of their homes."

**

"Women, break the wall of rigidity and achieve your goals."

**

"Women today need not play victims to become well-known."

**

"Women of today need a little push to run towards their goals."

**

*"The women of today are gorgeous from the
inside to the outside."*

**

"All women of today ought to write their own inspirational stories."

**

"Women pay attention: Stay how you are, and learn to love yourself."

**

"Women today know how to fight for themselves without anyone's help."

**

"Women of Today: Recite the mantra **"Me First"** every day in your life."

**

"Women of Today: If they regain their confidence, they are true winners."

**

"Women are born to lead their destinies. They are not here to be left behind."

**

"*The silence of women is not their weakness.
It is the most potent weapon ever.*"

**

"*Women are strong pillars both inside their homes and
outside their comfort zone.*"

**

"*Women need to be better than they already are to be
appreciated more by society.*"

**

"*Love yourself in the first place, women.
Then, dedicate yourself to your ambitions.*"

**

"*Women are powerful in their mental state.
They do not crumble under the sun or rain.*"

**

"*Stay away from the silence of women.
It can erupt at any moment to swallow you.*"

**

"Women are not aware of their hidden wings. So they are taking time to fly on their own."

**

"Today's women have gradually understood to care for themselves before caring for others."

**

"Women are the creators of the universe. They can also be its destroyers if they are bruised."

**

"If a woman can admire herself without a tinge of guilt, then she has truly arrived in her world."

**

"Women keep silent even in today's time. But it might be their strength instead of their weakness."

**

"Whatever women in today's world dream, they try to accomplish. That's their natural bend of mind."

**

"Women should speak for themselves because they can better convey their thoughts through words."

**

"Women are born warriors; Give them the swords of trust; they will win any battle that comes their way."

**

"Women should oppose 'wrongdoings', 'oppression', 'mental pressure', 'ego', and 'negativity' in their lives."

**

"Women of today have multiple talents, but what makes them strong are the invisible scars they silently carry."

**

"Society tutors women's minds from birth to act vulnerable. But, in reality, women are not fragile at all from within."

**

'Women need respect from society. If they cannot give it to the women, society should not expect it from them either."

**

"Women are fully aware of their potential only now. So, women of today, rise from the deep slumber of ignorance!"

**

"We train a woman to fly high in the sky. But we clip her wings when she gets elevated and begins to fly. How ironic is that!"

**

"Women do not require mentors to guide them in their lives. They are themselves the guiding lights that shows the path to others."

**

"Why should women compromise and sacrifice their own joy for others' happiness? Let others take that responsibility from now on."

**

"Women love their families more than anyone loves them. However, they will destroy everything if they get hurt beyond a limitation."

**

"Every home is incomplete without a woman residing within it. Encourage her to handle your home and heart. She is here to rule the universe in the end."

**

"Do not imprison me with your judgment. It will neither make me your slave nor restrict my progress. I will soar high in the sky even without your approval. Loose the knot before I strive to break free from your shackles." **Through a woman's mind**

**

"Women have the potential to compose their own stories. They can be the director of their life's account. They are also competent enough to execute their roles to perfection."

**

Mother

"Mother is not a label but an emotion."

**

"Mothers are the rarest species in the entire world."

**

"Babies are blessings by the Almighty for mothers."

**

"A mother's lap is the safest cocoon for a child of any age."

**

"The mother has no retirement plans. She is consistently at work with no pay."

**

"Only a mother can understand her children wholeheartedly like nobody else."

**

"Mother is not only a single endearing individual but a collection of emotions."

**

"There is always an invisible energy behind everyone's success in life. It belongs to a mother."

**

"A mother can never retire from her role in life. She gives her blessing even in her afterlife stage."

**

"You can love your mother wholeheartedly or be rude to her. But you can never overlook her in your life."

**

"What does a mother call it when she forgets to enjoy freely? Does she call it sacrifice or love for her children?"

**

"A mother's emotions are like the seven colours of a rainbow in life. When they are mixed, love oozes out of it without an end."

**

"A woman's life takes a 360-degree turn after a baby is born. She becomes a mother, a protector, a friend, a guide, and a confidante for the rest of her life."

**

Teachers

"Good teachers are rare jewels in today's world."

**

"Teachers act as guiding lights in this dark society."

**

"Teachers are the epitome of wisdom and reverence."

**

"A learned person is only sometimes the best teacher."

**

"Teachers are the guiding lights on the path of darkness."

**

"A teacher can build one's profession or destroy one's life."

**

"A good teacher listens to the silliest of babbles from a student."

**

"A person eager to learn at every step of life
is a dedicated teacher."

**

"A person who is better at comprehending an issue than you is known as a teacher."

**

"The teacher is the only mentor who can permanently boost or hinder a student's progress."

**

"He who guides and rectifies his mistakes daily is better known as a teacher. You are the best teacher in the universe who continuously refines yourself to improve every waking moment of yours."

**

"The world needs to acknowledge the work of good teachers. The teachers will then nurture future talents without any complaint."

**

"A teacher needs always to take questions from his students. Even when he or she might be exhausted or running out of time."

**

"A darkness of ignorance would prevail in the world without the steady candle of wisdom illuminated by dedicated teachers."

**

Friendship

"One's real friend is her most trusted therapist in life."

**

"Friendship survives through the most challenging times."

**

"Each friend resides on a different page in our life's book."

**

"Friendship is an emotion I feel every moment of my life."

**

"A third person can never enter between two close friends."

**

"Life will only be so appealing with friends who are family."

**

"Friends give the weirdest advice when you do not need them."

**

"A real friend understands and accepts you with your true self."

**

"Friends are the most valuable treasure one can possess in life."

**

"Good neighbours are hard to find today, just like good friends."

**

"I enjoy gossiping 24X7 with my friends when the topic is not me."

**

"Friends are the wealth one can depend upon and utilise at any time."

**

"Friendship is an addiction where friends do not yearn to be de-addicted."

**

"Friends fight over trivial issues with you but can fight for you with others."

**

"BFF: Best Friend Forever

It is rare to discover one in today's world. Do not let them go if you find one."

**

"Friends are similar to sugar syrup. They bring sweetness to every bitter recipe in life."

**

"Friends never leave your side in any situation. If they do, then they are not your friend at all."

**

"The difference in age, time, language, or distance can never be a hindrance to true friendship."

**

"A genuine friend has the latest update about you even if they have not spoken to you recently."

**

"Friends come as a complete assortment for you. They are full of drama, comedy, suspense, and love."

**

"One cannot overlook friends or stay annoyed with them for long. Because they are your buddies, and both of you need each other."

**

"Friendship is the invisible thread where multiple friends are bound together like strings in a necklace. Therefore, each bead represents one buddy staying close to the other."

**

Siblings

"Siblings are your first playmates and confidants. After some years, the role reverses. Friends transform into siblings. All in one family: You, siblings, and friends."

**

"Siblings are the leaves of the same tree, bound by love."

**

"When one knows that their siblings will love them till the last breath. It's their lifetime insurance."

**

"Being there for your brother or sister is the highest treasure in life."

**

"They fight like cats and dogs all the time.
They annoy each other like no one else can.
But they cannot survive without each other.
They are called siblings."

**

"You can sometimes be the most annoying sibling, yet you are lovable."

**

"One unique thread, smeared with love and affection, links sibling's hearts throughout their lives and is better known as Rakhi".

**

"Brothers and sisters have an unspoken agreement to support each other regardless of what the circumstances are."

**

"Why do you need anyone when you have your small army of brothers and sisters?"

**

"The original partner-in-crime in the world is one's brother or sister. Nobody can take their position at any cost in life."

**

Parents

"Parents' love for a child is the purest and most flawless one.
Home is where parents reside, and it is heaven on Earth."

**

"Fathers love their children without much expectation. However,
society must also recognise their sacrifice and love towards their
children."

**

"Parents are the guiding lights of every child."

**

"Parents are the stable backbone of every child."

**

"Babies transform one's life into magical moments.
They are the most precious joy for their parents and their homes."

**

"Love and respect your parents, irrespective of
their income and age."

**

"Dads fulfil their duty without openly exhibiting their
love and appreciation for their children."

**

"Dads are silent heroes in the real world for their children."

**

Children

"Children are the magnets of a family."

**

*"A baby completes a home to the fullest.
It makes a home sunny and the happiest place in the world."*

**

"A baby lights up the entire house with its toothless smile."

**

*"Why does a baby look radiant and happy all the time?
It's because the baby has no ego, not a drop of doubt,
or added stress in life."*

**

"Children teach us valuable life lessons every day."

**

*"The country's tomorrow lies in the hands of its children.
So encourage them and let them create a better nation."*

**

"Each child is unparalleled."

**

"Babies look like the most innocent thing in the world when they are sleeping."

**

"Children need freedom and love. If provided with those, they will blossom into gorgeous flowers."

**

"Children have genuine hearts and uncomplicated minds. They do not discriminate between the poor and the rich."

**

"Every child's superhero is their father. They always keep the image of their father in their mind even after they grow up."

**

"A baby's mind and life are like a blank canvas. Colour them with immense love and care."

**

"A new born baby in its mother's lap is the most loving frame of a photograph ever."

**

"Children are the future of a country.
Prepare them to be the leaders of tomorrow.
Age should not be a hindrance in progression."

**

"Let the children explore and discover the world on their own.
They will uncover more opportunities and make better creations
than the adults."

**

Family

"Where one's heart lies is family."

**

"Family is a blend of trust, affection, support, and enjoyment."

**

"Each individual has their family's strong backing in good and bad times."

**

"The family is a link where everyone lives with love and harmony."

**

"Neighbours become an extended family when your own family is not around you."

**

"Family plays an integral part in everyone's life. You can love or hate your family, but never forget it."

**

"Spending time with family and friends during any festival is the actual celebration."

**

Section-C

Patience

"Patience leads to performing better in life."

**

"A patient man is the wealthiest man in the world."

**

"One's patience in life can lead to hitting the jackpot in the end."

**

"Patience is the key to success. One may face failure if they falter and become impatient."

**

"Patience is an amalgamation of Power, Virtue, and self-control. They are the true strengths of any human being."

**

Kindness

131

"Keep sporting the attire of kindness throughout your life."

**

"Kindness begins at your doorstep but ends in others' hearts."

**

"Kindness is the coveted gift that costs nothing
yet gives back a lot."

**

"Kindness or being kind costs nothing. But behaving rudely, and
you lose many things."

**

"Kindness never goes wasted. It comes back to reward you.
Spread the act of kindness."

**

"A small portion of kindness thrown to the world spreads
immense blessings everywhere."

**

"Kindness is contagious in its fashion. It spreads to places where your eyes cannot even reach."

**

"Being kind to others is a forever encouraging deed. But make sure that others don't take advantage of it."

**

"An act of kindness never goes unappreciated. The reward for it comes back to you in one form or the other."

**

Hope

"Our life goes on through hope."

**

"Hope is the first ray in everyday life."

**

"The fragrance of the "Hope" flower spreads until immensity and never fades."

**

"The light that is eternally luminous in the heart is hope. There is no darkness in the path of hope."

**

Trust

"Trust nobody, not even yourself."

**

"Every bond in the universe is joined by trust."

**

"Trust is gradually built by patience in silence."

**

"Trusting someone without much thought is an act of fearlessness."

**

"Trusting is similar to gambling. You win or you lose in a relationship."

**

"Trust and love are two sides of the same coin. One cannot exist without the other."

**

"Trust is the most precious piece of jewellery that cannot be found again once lost."

**

Happiness

"Inner happiness is reflected on the face."

**

"Happiness is a state of mind. Stay happy every moment in life."

**

"Experience the rain of happiness and compassion
every single day."

**

"Good intentions and the right actions lead
to happiness via success."

**

"Happiness is a contagious condition;
It spreads quickly like a forest fire."

**

"Happiness is found in the inner store of one's soul and not in outer worldly stores."

**

"Happiness is similar to a colourful bubble.
It may burst at any moment, even with a tender caress."

**

"Suppressed emotions and happiness explode without warning.
Either in the form of tears or an outburst of words."

**

Success

"Perseverance is the key to success."

**

"Work in silence to inscribe your success story."

**

"Success is ours when we overcome our worries."

**

"A dedicated routine in daily life leads to success."

**

"Success is an ongoing journey. It is not the final destination."

**

"Overcome your imperfections and stride towards your success."

**

"The path to success goes through perseverance and consistency."

**

"A tiny seed of a belief flourishes into a successful
business over time."

**

"Humbleness is the key to success. It runs in the blood of every person."

**

"Behind every success story, a lot of strength, sacrifice, sincerity, and silence prevails."

**

"Five keys to unlock success: Determination, discipline, rejection, belief, and diligence."

**

"Success and failure are two sides of the same coin. When one is upward, the other lies south."

**

"Consistency in work is the key to success. A relevant lesson we learned from Mahatma Gandhi."

**

"Every successful person is hard-working. But only some hard-working personalities are successful."

**

Respect

"A respected man is the wealthiest man in the society."

**

"Respect should be earned and not demanded from others."

**

"Appreciate others in the same manner you wish to be respected."

**

"Respect and love yourself first before showing respect to others."

**

"It takes ages to earn respect, yet it takes minutes to lose respect in other's eyes."

**

"Do not waste money and time on those who do not display a little respect for you."

**

Silence

"Silence can be deadly at times."

**

"Silence is the highest mantra for a happy life."

**

"Silence is the blessing from God in the hour of distress."

**

"Silent people are good listeners, and they make best friends."

**

"Being silent is not beneficial in some events. You need to communicate to clarify misunderstandings."

**

"Keeping silent neither erases trauma nor pain in the long run. One ought to voice their abuse and fight for their rights."

**

Section-D

Love

"Love can transform the world."

**

"Love is not a game of musical chairs.
If unoccupied, then anyone can take the chair."

**

"Love is the most pleasant and intangible emotion in life."

**

"Transmit love and care to the cosmos and fetch
sweet surprises from it."

**

"Love is the most beautiful emotion. Love yourself first
and then the world."

**

"Fate gives wounds to the body, time heals the mind,
and love soothes the soul."

**

"Falling in love is easy. Holding that love forever in your
heart is the toughest part."

**

Heartbreak

"A broken heart is forever lethal."

**

"Is breakup right or wrong? It depends upon the circumstances."

**

"The infringement of the heart delivers the most shattering sound."

**

"Once broken, only fragments lay scattered around. Be it a heart or glass."

**

"Let a breakup make you stronger than before. Let it not shatter your dreams in life."

**

"Breakups do not always make one sad. They can also sometimes clear the mind's clutter."

**

"Life does not end after a bitter separation. No matter how painful the breakup is, life goes on."

**

"A shattered heart after a breakup produces the most deafening noise. Have the patience to endure the discomfort for a while."

**

Mental Health

"Depression is similar to a furious downpour.
Staying calm is the best choice during that time."

**

"One invisible foe that dwells within our minds is depression.
Neither disregard it nor be attentive towards it."

**

"An overambitious nature and uncertain expectations drive one
to a world of depression."

**

"There is a thin line between loneliness and depression.
One wrong move and one plunge into a disastrous space."

**

"It is not wise to nurture the seed of melancholy.
As it will turn into a tree of depression in the future."

**

"Depression slowly takes the life out of people."

**

"Grief, anxiety, misery, and impairment are accumulated in the subconscious with time. Then it gushes out in the form of either tears or rage."

**

"Depression is more like one's own shadow.
It sticks to you 24x7, 365 days.
But you should not let it overpower your subconscious."

**

"Mental illness is taken less seriously than physical illness.
But it can be life-threatening if it is not treated on time."

**

"Depressed people are not conscious of their plight."

**

"Depression has not been anyone's choice since the beginning.
There is no substantial evidence for: 'Why,' 'How,' or 'when' of
this state of depression."

**

"Depression, mental illness, and feeling low are today's new
diseases. They're more complicated than we imagine them to be."

**

Addiction

"An addiction of any form is like one's shadow."

**

"Convert your addiction into your passion."

**

"An addiction can take you either to the path
of victory or tragedy."

**

"The source of intoxication can differ from person to person.
Be it power, money, knowledge, entertainment, or alcohol."

**

"Addiction is not always about alcohol, drugs, or nicotine."

**

"There is no fatal infection in life like an addiction to anything."

**

"Drunk people commit offences in their sound
mind but cleverly blame alcohol."

**

"People who often find their comfort in alcohol also
find mathematics complicated."

**

"Intoxicated people pose a serious threat to society."

**

"Beware of all intoxicated people in the universe. They are blind
in their actions."

**

"In the journey of addiction, no family or friend will accompany
you. Instead, you will wander alone on the path, either towards
freedom or confinement for your entire life."

**

"Alcohol does not help solve problems in life. Instead,
it creates more trouble."

**

"One shot of tequila and your work stress is out of the window."

**

"When life gives you alcohol, make a martini and enjoy the sunset because impaired thinking is best enjoyed by doing nothing."

**

"The addiction to Alcohol is the root cause of many crimes."

**

"Addiction and obsession are two sides of a coin called demolition in life."

**

"Drinking a glass of wine with crackers alone is more fun than sitting and chattering with a group of indifferent people."

**

Apologies

"The mightiest weapon of a word, 'Sorry,' has been misused for years."

**

"Sorry is an expensive word in today's world."

**

"Saying sorry is like having a cup of coffee. It fixes everything instantly."

**

"The word 'Sorry' loses its significance if used frequently."

**

"Sorry is the most powerful emotion. It is told in a thousand ways to multiple people in numerous circumstances."

**

"Sorry is an integral part of our lives. One cannot survive without it."

**

Marriage

"The secret ingredient to a successful marriage is sticking together under all circumstances and allowing no space for others to enter a couple's life."

**

"The most flawed personalities flourish in marriage."

**

"There is a saying that 'Marriages are made in Heaven.' So are rain and snow."

**

"Perfect companions and flawless weddings are a myth in life."

**

"Every wedding depicts a unique story."

**

"Husband and wife: Two wheels of a cycle called life."

**

"Wedding is similar to gambling. You lose everything and be miserable or win to get addicted for a lifetime."

**

"There is no perfect relationship status between spouses in a marriage. Life sails without a hitch if one accepts their spouse with all of their flaws."

**

"The relationship between a husband and a wife is always unpredictable."

**

"Marriage is a blend of joy and sorrow."

**

"Problems between a husband and wife also exist in a perfect marriage."

**

"Every husband's strength lies in his wife's smile. Likewise, every wife dreams of seeing her husband's support in each of her decisions."

**

Independence

"A rationally independent person believes in himself first."

**

"True independence is an emotional and mental exercise, along with some physical movement."

**

"The fearless heart unlocks the door of independence."

**

"When we are free from negativity and fear of defeat, then independence will embrace us in the true sense."

**

"If a single thought arising from me is accomplished without any exterior influence or hindrance, it's independence for me."

**

"Freedom is a state of mind. We are prisoners of our minds. Break free from the mind's prison to inhale the refreshing air of freedom."

**

Money

"I love my best buddy – money.
However, it does not think the same way."

**

"Money either creates problems or solves issues."

**

"Money is the greatest manipulator of all time."

**

"Money is a source of distress for human beings."

**

"My mind constantly tells me to contribute money to other needy
people. I have started the mission with myself first."

**

"Money lost in life will come back today or tomorrow.
However, lost time can never be recovered."

**

"Preserve money for rainy days, i.e., for unforeseen mishaps."

**

"Money is no longer a luxury.
It is now an essentiality."

**

"Work hard to make money. Do not run after it or around it."

**

"Money can shape or ruin a relationship.
Be cautious around it."

**

"All successful people earn money.
However, not everyone who earns money is successful."

**

"Money is an inevitable requirement throughout one's entire
life."

**

"The quest for earning money is endless."

**

"If one cannot control their money, they will be in trouble."

**

"Money comes handy in times of crisis."

**

"Money destroys many connections if not utilised judiciously."

**

"Money is a great friend as well as a harsh foe in life."

**

"Money and success change every relationship over time."

**

"Money is not always the origin of devastation.
It can be the source of happiness in life too."

**

Section-E

Dance

"Through every dance performance, the dancer narrates a tale."

**

"Dancers express their emotions through their dance movements."

**

"Life resembles a dance podium where we dance to the tunes of the creator of the universe."

**

"Dance is salvation for several folks. Embrace the art form with passion."

**

"Dancers can sway their bodies without external music. Because they have built-in music within themselves."

**

"If dance is your love, go and learn it. Nobody can stop you from dancing, not even you."

**

"Dance is a holistic movement of body and mind."

**

"*Dancers express their emotions through the art of dancing.*"

**

"*Inner emotions flow out rhythmically from dancers through the form of dance.*"

**

"*Dancers are never lonely.*
They dance to their own tune."

**

"*D - Dreams*
A - Are
N - Never
C - Controlled by
E - Emotions."

**

Art & Books

"Books are like a good addiction for book lovers."

**

"Books cling on to you, listen to you, and even initiate a conversation with you out of the blue."

**

"Books are the most loyal friends forever.
They never leave your side or backstab you."

**

"Books cling to you more than your loved ones, patiently listen to your rambling, and even strike up a conversation with you out of the blue."

**

"Books guide one to the entrance of the knowledge world.
Enjoy your visit to the land of books at least once in your lifetime!"

**

"Art is an intrinsic element of our life."

**

"Artists think differently from the common crowd."

**

*"Poetry is an expression of emotions that flows
out from the heart."*

**

*"Creativity is born out of motivation. It doesn't matter whether
it takes shape from within the artist or from an outside source."*

**

Travel

"Travel to broaden your horizon of compassion and unpretentiousness."

**

"Make time to travel with your loved ones."

**

"Travellers are the best storytellers in the world. They have remarkable eyes and sharp ears for their captions."

**

"Travelling is the best mentor. It reveals life teachings that we do not find in any book."

**

"Travelling, Travellers, and Travel destinations are distinctive elements of life."

**

"One has to lose inhibition to explore different places through travelling."

**

"Travelling broadens one's horizons and expands it to infinity."

**

"Travel unfolds hidden stories from numerous travellers."

**

"Travel rewards you with a new you,
That you were not aware of yourself."

**

"Travel to an unknown destination to discover its rich knowledge."

**

"Step out of your comfort zone for travelling.
You will meet a new you after the journey."

**

"Never travel to spend money or as a sign of social status.
Instead, travel exclusively to create a new experience."

**

"Traveling is more beneficial than obtaining bookish
information."

**

"Traveling gives more profound knowledge than books."

**

"The most significant adventure in life is to come out of one's comfort zone to travel alone."

**

"Travelling is an ongoing journey in your life."

**

"Traveling to new places as a traveller is a part of one's life."

**

"Travelling is the key that opens the door of zeal, insight, and composure."

**

"Fill the moments of your travel with happiness. The experience will be locked in your memory forever."

**

"Travel is an eye-opener for all sorts of tourists.
One may gain vast knowledge and become modest while
Others may show off their money and be arrogant."

**

"Traveling is a lifetime experience."

**

"Travelling is the world's most reliable therapy."

**

"It's always possible to travel and enjoy different places."

**

*"Travelling is an ongoing adventure.
There is no ultimate destination."*

**

"There are no limitations to travelling."

**

"Travelling is a compilation of incredible memories."

**

Anti-War

"War gives nothing other than pain."

**

"War is the warehouse of wreckage."

**

"War leaves nothing but trails of devastation."

**

"War never solves a problem. Instead, it creates
thousands of them."

**

"War is never worthwhile for humanity.
It shatters harmony and swallows peace."

**

Country & Language

"All languages are born from the heart."

**

"The hospitality shown to others is any country's identity."

**

"India is predominant in terms of heritage and intellectual mind."

**

"Indians are deeply connected through their love for their country."

**

*"India stands for **Iconic, Notable, Diverse, Innovative,** and **Aesthetic** Nation."*

**

"Every country should always be proud of their country and respect its people."

**

"Hindustan's soul rests in the Hindi language. Stay connected to this rich dialect."

**

"Celebrating Hindi Diwas makes us realise the importance of the language in our lives."

**

"India gained its independence because of the sacrifices of countless people. Let us not disregard it ever."

**

"Any country's progress depends upon the popularity of the commoner's language rather than any foreign language."

**

"We should show respect to our country for giving us independence. Moreover, we should be grateful to the people who made it possible."

**

Perfection

"I do not intend to be perfect anymore.
I have chosen my role model – it's me."

**

"Perfection is the master of unhappiness."

**

"The road to perfection is slippery many times."

**

"To achieve perfectionism is the mother of all misery."

**

"Do not run after the perfection mirage.
It will not help to quench your thirst for fulfilment."

**

"Nobody can attain the perfect state in one's lifetime,
as it is a relative term in the real world."

**

Section-F

Festivals

"Diwali is a celebration of lights with sweets."

**

"A day when the darkness of ignorance gives way to the light of enlightenment is known as Diwali."

**

"This Diwali, expel these negative qualities from life:
D-Darkness of Failure
I- Ignorance of Myths
W-Weight of Error
A- Anxiety for the Future
L- Lies of Mind
I-Ingenious Of Deceptions."

**

"Let the smile on your face light up, like a million Diyas, this Deepavali!"

**

"The festivals are meant for merriment and fun, not shattered with noise and bloodshed."

**

"Dussehra is a festival of positivity, a ceremony to celebrate achievement, and a day full of bliss."

**

"Rath Yatra is not just a festival. It is an emotional bond between Lord Jagannath and his devotees."

**

"Holi is the festival where we can see the rainbow shades in every corner."

**

"H-Humanity

O-Optimism

L-Laughter

I-Integrity

Holi elevates the spirit of happiness!"

**

"Dussehra constantly mentions the victory of good over evil."

**

"We should fill the water pitcher with colours of reverence, laughter, friendship, integrity and emotions during Holi."

**

"Every day is portrayed in black and white throughout the year. Only one day is reserved for colours – the day of Holi."

**

"Let the colour of optimism blend with the colours of Holi to spread happiness in life."

**

"Every festival is filled with optimism, compassion, miracles, and gratitude."

**

"Let the splash of colours remove the negativity from life and envelop everyone with joy on the day of Holi!"

**

"Christmas is not merely a festival. It's full of high energy and happiness."

**

"Santa, Reindeer, blessings, surprise gifts, a Christmas tree, and endless goodies make Christmas merrier and more joyful."

**

"Christmas is a symbol of merrymaking and exuberance."

**

"Deity, demon, devotion, Dussehra, destroy, dream, and death. These are the real elements of Dussehra."

**

New Year

"The days of a new year resemble the blank pages of a diary."

**

"Do not look back to the year that has passed. Learn the lessons
it has taught. Leap towards the New Year with extra vigour,
hope, and happiness."

**

"A new year is only a sum of 365 days.
Every day is a new one filled with hope and happiness."

**

"One should always begin the New Year refreshed, with renewed
optimism, confidence, and positive energy."

**

"Let the New Year be the beginning of a new you."

**

"New Year symbolises new days ahead for you.
Let go of the old days; catch the new options."

**

"New Year: New You: New Resolutions."

**

"The New Year brings new hope to everyone's life."

**

"New Year brings new hope for some.
However, it may be trivial for others."

**

"New Year, New Resolution, New Opportunity,
but you are still the same."

**

"New Year is like an empty record to write down new stories. It
may be exemplary ones or terrible experiences."

**

"Leave the disappointments behind in the previous year.
Embrace the new options that stand before you in the New
Year."

**

213

"N- Nothing Is

E- Envisioned

W- Without

Y- Your

E- Enthusiastic

A- Approach to

R- Resolve Old Problems"

**

"New Year is similar to a blank cheque.

Fill the space with contentment.

Then, deposit it in life's account."

**

Birthday

*"Birthdays are gentle reminders to perform better
and to fret less."*

**

*"Birthdays are excuses to get wild for a day.
Then, blame it entirely on the birthday."*

**

*"Birthdays are a reminder of one's accomplishments
and failures."*

**

*"A birthday is invariably filled with laughter, happiness,
gifts, feasts, and dresses."*

**

*"Every birthday is an unforgettable day.
Immerse yourself in the blessings, love, and wishes showered upon you."*

**

"One's Birthday is a reminder of one's existence in the world."

**

"Birthdays are a joyous experience for all, irrespective of age."

**

"Birthdays are like one's life book. One attaches another new
page to it on every birthday celebration."

**

"We wait 364 days to enjoy our birthday. Then, the day after
the celebration, we again start counting the days for the next."

**

"The special day called birthday carries one close
to one's mission in life."

**

Mornings

"Every morning is the doorway to a momentous day."

**

"Everything shines when one creates a bright morning."

**

"We should pray to the Almighty every morning without fail to remove all our distress from our lives."

**

"May a thousand hearts get illuminated every morning with your radiant smile!"

**

"The morning will transform into a beautiful day if we pray, smile, and be good to others."

**

"Each day brings a new success or failure in life."

**

"We should reload our minds with fresh ideas every morning."

**

"The new day brings new aspirations, invigorated energy, and fresh thoughts to fill our 24-hour empty book."

**

"Mornings are the beginnings of a unique phase in everyday life. They can be good, harsh, or uncertain. Just live through the day."

**

"Each morning is high in energy. Inhale the positive power and discard the negative vibes."

**

"Every morning provides you with extra energy. Feel good about it and soak in its beauty."

**

"Every new morning is filled with golden rays, bringing hope for the new day."

**

"Each morning begins with a new assortment of optimism, beginning, and energy."

**

"A morning cup filled with blessings and good thoughts makes the day beautiful."

**

"Each morning should begin with prayers.
So that every night ends with a miracle."

**

"Every morning leads the way to a new day.
Be happy with it!"

**

"Wish yourself a good morning every day without fail.
The life will appear bright every morning."

**

"Optimism has expanded over the morning sky to make it more charming and enjoyable."

**

"Each morning looks bright and beautiful because you are going to make it worthy.

So count your blessings every morning!"

**

"Smile at others, pray to the Almighty, and show gratitude to the world first thing in the morning."

**

"Every morning should be a good day for you, regardless of the circumstances."

**

"Every new morning gives us unlimited blessings, which, in turn, gives us hope to renew our life every day."

**

Dreams

"Accomplish the dreams that you have envisioned for yourself. It will be the most incredible experience of your entire life."

**

"Give everyone the strength to accomplish their dreams by overcoming their weaknesses."

**

"Dreams have wings, and they fly away quickly. Catch them before it is too late to realise their importance."

**

"My dreams are endless in my emotions."

**

"Dreams transform into existence through consistent determination."

**

"There might be a hundred reasons to stay unhappy. However, there will always be one reason to be happy."

**

"Fantasies shape dreams."

**

Goodbye

"A goodbye can be a boon or hang as a curse on you."

**

"The person who dares to say goodbye is the most courageous."

**

"Goodbyes are never effortless, either for the departed
or for those left behind."

**

"Goodbye does not always indicate despair.
Sometimes, it is a solace to say goodbye."

**

"Goodbyes are often disheartening.
It can either relieve your pain or leave you in a lurch."

**

Milton Keynes UK
Ingram Content Group UK Ltd.
UKHW040819250224
438359UK00001B/11

9 789359 895192